# Counting by: Threes

## Esther Sarfatti

Rourke
Publishing LLC
Vero Beach, Florida 32964

www.rourkepublishing.com

PHOTO CREDITS: © Eileen Hart: title page and pages 5 and 21; © Jean Frooms: page 3; © James Steidl: page 7; © Christine Balderas: page 9; © Ramona Heim: page 11; © Jason Lugo: page 13; © Michael Ledray: page 19; © Terry Reimink: page 23.

Editor: Robert Stengard-Olliges

Cover design by Nicola Stratford.

**Library of Congress Cataloging-in-Publication Data**

Sarfatti, Esther.
 Counting by : threes / Esther Sarfatti.
   p. cm. -- (Concepts)
 ISBN 978-1-60044-523-1 (Hardcover)
 ISBN 978-1-60044-664-1 (Softcover)
 1.  Counting--Juvenile literature.  I. Title.
  QA113.S3563 2008
  513.2'11--dc22
                                    2007014071

Printed in the USA

CG/CG

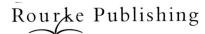

Rourke Publishing

www.rourkepublishing.com – rourke@rourkepublishing.com
Post Office Box 3328, Vero Beach, FL 32964

# This is three.

What comes in threes?

Three **3**

**3** Three

Three **3**

5

A traffic light has three lights.

7

A tricycle has three wheels.

9

A triangle has three sides.

This flag has three colors.

This clownfish has three stripes.

This sundae has three scoops.

This lizard has three horns.

19

This family has three kids.

21

These three kids are triplets.
Counting by threes is fun!

23

# Index

**Further Reading**

Fitzkee, Jeremy. *One, Two, Three, Me*. Viking Penguin, 2006.
Jacobson, David. *Three Wishes*. Sterling, 2006.

**Recommended Websites**

www.edhelper.com/kindergarten/Number_3.htm
www.enchantedlearning.com/languagebooks/spanish/numbers/

**About the Author**

Esther Sarfatti has worked with children's books for over 15 years as an editor and translator. This is her first series as an author. Born in Brooklyn, New York, and brought up in a trilingual home, Esther currently lives with her husband and son in Madrid, Spain.